THE DEATH OF SUPERMAN

DAN JURGENS
JERRY ORDWAY
LOUISE SIMONSON
ROGER STERN

WRITERS

JON BOGDANOVE
TOM GRUMMETT
JACKSON GUICE
DAN JURGENS

PENCILLERS

BRETT BREEDING
RICK BURCHETT
DOUG HAZLEWOOD
DENNIS JANKE
DENIS RODIER

INKERS

JOHN COSTANZA
ALBERT DEGUZMAN
BILL OAKLEY
WILLIE SCHUBERT

LETTERERS

GENE D'ANGELO
GLENN WHITMORE

COLORISTS

SUPERMAN created by
JERRY SIEGEL **and** JOE SHUSTER
By Special arrangement with the JERRY SIEGEL **family**

MIKE CARLIN, BRIAN AUGUSTYN
Editors – Original Series

JENNIFER FRANK, RUBEN DIAZ
Assistant Editors – Original Series

BOB KAHAN
Editor

ROBBIN BROSTERMAN
Design Director – Books

SARABETH KETT
Publication Design

BOB HARRAS
Senior VP – Editor-in-Chief, DC Comics

DIANE NELSON
President

DAN DIDIO AND JIM LEE
Co-Publishers

GEOFF JOHNS
Chief Creative Officer

AMIT DESAI
Senior VP – Marketing and Franchise Management

AMY GENKINS
Senior VP – Business and Legal Affairs

NAIRI GARDINER
Senior VP – Finance

JEFF BOISON
VP – Publishing Planning

MARK CHIARELLO
VP – Art Direction and Design

JOHN CUNNINGHAM
VP – Marketing

TERRI CUNNINGHAM
VP – Editorial Administration

LARRY GANEM
VP – Talent Relations and Services

ALISON GILL
Senior VP – Manufacturing and Operations

HANK KANALZ
Senior VP – Vertigo and Integrated Publishing

JAY KOGAN
VP – Business and Legal Affairs, Publishing

JACK MAHAN
VP – Business Affairs, Talent

NICK NAPOLITANO
VP – Manufacturing Administration

SUE POHJA
VP – Book Sales

FRED RUIZ
VP – Manufacturing Operations

COURTNEY SIMMONS
Senior VP – Publicity

BOB WAYNE
Senior VP – Sales

SOMEWHERE ELSE...

KRAANG!

KRAANG!

KRAANG!

>KRAANG!<

...DOOMSDAY IS COMING!

UNRELENTINGLY...

KRAANG!

KRAANG!

KRAANG!

KRIINK!

....DOOMSDAY IS COMING!

UNBELIEVABLY...

KRAANG!

KRAANG!

KRAANG!

KROOM

...DOOMSDAY IS HERE!

DOOMSDAY!

PART ONE

STORY : LOUISE SIMONSON
PENCILLER : JON BOGDANOVE
INKER : DENNIS JANKE
LETTERER : BILL OAKLEY
COLORIST : GLENN WHITMORE
ASSISTANT : JENNIFER FRANK
EDITOR : MIKE CARLIN

SUPERMAN created by
JERRY SIEGEL & JOE SHUSTER

HE'S SO... AWESOME! HE SAVED ME... TWO TIMES NOW. HE'S MY FRIEND.

·I WISH I COULD TELL HIM... BUT... I JUST CAN'T.

MAXALEH'S HARDWARE

OPEN PLEASE COME IN

HOURS

KEYS MA

WHILE U W

ARMOR LOCK

SO THERE'S ONLY ONE THING LEFT TA DO.

CHAN·L·OCK

FLEISCHER · PAI
INTERIOR / EXT · CUSTOM
ENAMEL & FLA BLENDED

YOU SURE THIS PAINT REALLY GLOWS IN THE DARK?

YEAH. LATEST THING. GUARANTEED.

SAY, YOU AIN'T PLANNIN' TA USE IT ON ANY SUBWAY WALLS, ARE YA, KID?

NO. 'COURSE NOT.

AT LEAST... NOT EXACTLY.

HARDWARE

KEYS MAKE

FLUORESCEN YELLO

I'M SCARED. BUT I GUESS IT MAKES SENSE TA BE SCARED--

ELSEWHERE...

SCANNED THE CITY, BUT DIDN'T SEE ANY UNDER-WORLDERS ON THE SURFACE.

MUST BE LYING LOW FOR NOW. MAYBE IT'S TIME --

HI, CLARK. LOIS LEFT YOU A COMPUTER MESSAGE.

"-- I GOT BACK TO WORK!"

VERY HIGH TECH OF HER. THANKS, FRAN.

TAK-TAP-TAK-TAP!

READ: MESSAGES

WHAT NOW?

ALL THE COMPUTERS DON'T WORK?

LIGHTS, EITHER!

DON'T TELL ME... WE'RE HAVING ANOTHER BLACKOUT?!

WE DO IT!

YEAAAA!

WE STEAL METROPOLIS'S ELECTRICITY!

NOW CITY IS HELPLESS... AND UNDERWORLD CAN KICK BUTT!

WHO *ARE* YOU? WHAT'S *GOING ON?* CHARLIE-- HOW *COULD* YOU?

IT *EASY*, REPORTER LADY, AN' *SMART*. YOU HELP TEACH CHARLIE, DIDN'T YOU?

HE SOCIETY'S *REJECT*... LIKE US ALL.

YOU WANT TO GIVE US *HANDOUTS!*

BUT *UNDER-WORLD* GOTS *WAR MACHINES* NOW... AN' WE *TAKE* WHAT WE *WANT!*

SHE MIGHT BE USEFUL AS A *HOSTAGE*, CLAW. BETTER BRING HER TO THE *BOSS.*

YOU *TEASE* HER, CHARLIE. YOU KNOW BOSS DON'T TAKE *PRISONERS!*

SHE BE *DEAD* 'FORE HOUR IS UP!

NO PRISONERS? BUT WHAT ABOUT MY *MOMMA?*

THEY... THEY NEVER *HAD* MY MOMMA! THEY *LIED* TO ME SO I WOULDN'T TALK!

I-I GUESS... I KNEW... ALL ALONG THEY DIDN'T HAVE HER. I JUST WANTED TO *BELIEVE...*

...THAT I COULD *FIND* HER... AN' *SAVE* HER...

...AN' MAKE HER *LOVE* ME.

ELSEWHERE...

KRAK KRAM!

KRAKK!

THE MONSTERS DON'T HAVE MY MOMMA.

THIS PROBABLY MEANS I'M NEVER GONNA FIND HER...

BUT THEY REALLY DO HAVE THAT REPORTER LADY.

THEY'RE GONNA KILL HER. AN' ATTACK THE CITY.

THAT'S REAL. I CAN STOP THAT. AN' THAT MEANS TELLIN' SUPERMAN--FAST!

IT'S AWFUL DARK UP HERE! WHERE ARE THE STREET LIGHTS?

I BET THE MONSTERS DID IT.

I READ HOW THEY USE A BAT SYMBOL TO CALL BATMAN. ONLY IT'S IN THE SKY...

FFSSSTT

...AN' THIS ONE'S ON THE GROUND.

FPSSSSSTT

IT'S ALL MY FAULT! IF I TOLD SUPERMAN, 'STEAD OF BELIEVIN' MONSTERS' LIES...

...HE WOULDA ALREADY STOPPED 'EM!

I JUST HOPE MY IDEA WORKS!

SUPERMAN! SUPERMAN! PLEASE PLEASE SEE THE SIGNAL!

KEITH?

SUPERMAN, IT'S YOU! I KNEW YOU'D COME!

THERE'S THIS REPORTER LADY IN THE TUNNELS! MONSTERS HAVE HER--

BWAAMF!

GOOD THING CLAWSTER...

...INVULNERABLE!

TK-TK! <SUPERMAN COMING FOR US!> TK-TK!

TK-TK! <ACTIVATE WAR MACHINES! NOW!> TK-TK!

SHRAKT!

MISSED MY CHANCE TO STOP THEM ONCE...

WON'T MAKE THAT MISTAKE AGAIN!

WHAKT!

⁚WHUFF!⁚ ⁚HUFF!⁚

⟨THAT--⟩

⟨--SMARTS!⟩

POUND!

KRAZZZZH!

WHAM

KRL'LI'S UNCONSCIOUS! THE BATTLE SEEMS TO BE GOING AGAINST US!

PERHAPS, AFTER ALL, DISCRETION WOULD BE THE BETTER PART OF VALOR!

COME BACK HERE, WAR WORLDER!

WHERE'S THE LADY REPORTER YOU'RE HOLDING CAPTIVE?

C-CAPTIVE? SURELY, SUPERMAN, YOU KNOW... WE WARWORLDERS DON'T TAKE CAPTIVES!

WHERE IS SHE?

CHARLIE TOOK HER TO THE EAST TUNNEL! BY NOW, SHE'S DEAD!

W-WHAT ARE YOU GOING TO DO?

POUND YOU UP TO YOUR NECK INTO THE ROCK FLOOR!

AND MAYBE, IF YOU'RE WRONG, I MIGHT JUST BOTHER TO DIG YOU OUT AGAIN!

THE *JAILS* ON THE SURFACE WON'T *HOLD* THESE GUYS!

WE'LL HOLD A *TRIAL* AND DEAL WITH THEM IN *UNDERWORLD.*

BUT... YOU DON'T HAVE TO *STAY* DOWN HERE, YOU KNOW.

THERE'S A PLACE FOR YOU AND YOUR FRIENDS IN *METROPOLIS.*

YOU *KIDDIN'*, RIGHT?

AIN'T NUTHIN' FOR *US* ON THE SURFACE, AN' CHARLIE AN' ME'RE HUMAN.

AN' IT'S NOT LIKE MY FRIENDS GOT *MARKETABLE SKILLS* OR NUTHIN'. NAH...

...WE JAWED 'BOUT IT BEFORE, AN' WE DECIDED TA STAY IN THE *TUNNELS.*

WHAT ABOUT *YOU*, *CHARLIE?*

I COULD TRY TO GET YOU A JOB AT THE *PLANET.* YOU'RE PRETTY GOOD AT FERRETING OUT *INFORMATION.*

THANKS, MISS LANE. BUT I'LL TAKE MY CHANCES HERE.

THEN... MAYBE YOU CAN BE OUR *UNDERWORLD CORRESPONDENT?*

DEAL!

YA KNOW, GRUB, THERE'S WORSE DOWN HERE THAN THE WAR-WORLDERS.

YOU THINK I SHOULD TELL 'EM... MY *DUTY* AS A *CORRESPONDENT* AN' ALL?

NAH, BLOOD-THIRST IS *OUR* PROBLEM. BUT IT'S GOOD TO KNOW IF WE CAN'T *HANDLE* 'IM...

...WE CAN CALL IN *SUPERMAN!*

26

28

MY ICE WILL MELT SOME OF THE BLAZE!

GOOD MOVE, ICE! THE REST OF US WILL TAKE CARE OF THE VICTIMS!

WE SURE APPRECIATE THE HELP, JUSTICE LEAGUERS! I'M WELL AWARE THAT *OHIO* IS OUT OF YOUR NORMAL AREA OF JURISDICTION--

WE MUST FIND THE BEAST.

I AGREE, BLOODWYND. EVERYBODY INTO THE BUG AND WE'LL BE ON OUR WAY.

GOSH, IT'S TOO BAD WE HAVE THIS EMERGENCY! I REALLY WANTED TO SEE TODAY'S EPISODE--

"--OF THE CAT GRANT SHOW."

WE'RE COMING TO YOU LIVE FROM ROOSEVELT HIGH WITH AN *INCREDIBLE* SHOW!

HE IS PERHAPS THE MOST CELEBRATED MAN OF OUR TIME! HE'S BEEN CALLED THE MAN OF TOMORROW--

--THE LAST SON OF KRYPTON AND THE MAN OF STEEL! BUT HE'S MOST APPROPRIATELY KNOWN AS--

"--SUPERMAN!"

YEAH!

YAYYY

CLAP CLAP

CLAP CLAP CLAP

KEEP YOUR EYES ON THE GROUND, PEOPLE! THE SOONER WE SPOT OUR MONSTER THE BETTER!

HEY, BEETLE, IF IT'S A REALLY COOL MONSTER MAYBE WE SHOULD CAPTURE IT--

--AND TAKE IT ON THE TALK-SHOW CIRCUIT FOR BIG BUCKS!

YOUR SENSE OF THE APPROPRIATE KNOWS NO LIMITS, BOOSTER.

IT TOOK YOU THIS LONG TO REALIZE THAT, BLOODWYND?

Uh-oh...LOOKS LIKE WE'VE FOUND OUR MAN'S TRAIL OF CRUMBS!

CHECK OUT THAT PATH OF DESTRUCTION!

THOSE TREES WEREN'T MOWED DOWN BY A COUPLE OF KIDS ON SKATE-BOARDS!

THIS IS TERRIBLE! SUCH POINT-LESS...NEEDLESS DEVASTATION!

LET'S JUST FIND THE SUCKERS AND KICK SOME BUTT!

I CAN'T THANK YOU ENOUGH FOR JOINING US HERE, SUPERMAN. INTERVIEWS WITH YOU ARE A TRUE RARITY!

I'VE ALWAYS FELT THAT IF AMERICANS ARE TO TRUST US, THEY HAVE TO KNOW US, MS. GRANT.

AND WITHOUT YOUR TRUST WE ARE NOT EFFECTIVE.

YOU'VE EXHIBITED PSYCHIC POWERS BEFORE, BLOODWYND. ANY CHANCE YOU CAN SCAN AHEAD AND TAP INTO THIS GUY'S MIND?

IT WILL BE DIFFICULT--

--BUT I CAN TRY.

AS WILL I--

I GUESS TWO PSYCHIC MINDS ARE BETTER THAN ONE.

NUTS! I WANTED BLOODWYND TO GO IT ALONE SO I'D HAVE A CHANCE TO GAUGE HIS POWERS!

IT'S THE ONLY WAY I CAN GET INFO ON THE GUY!

THE WAY HE SHIELDS HIS ABILITIES HE'LL PROBABLY LET MAXIMA MAKE FIRST CONTACT EVEN IF--

YES!

I'VE FOUND THE CREATURE!

HE'S HATE--

--DEATH AND BLOOD LUST PERSONIFIED!

NOTHING MORE.

34

IT'S UNFAIR TO THE OTHERS TO PAINT ME AS THE *LEADER* OF THE JUSTICE LEAGUE.

WE'RE A GROUP OF PEOPLE WHO HAVE GOTTEN TOGETHER TO DO A JOB ONLY WE CAN DO.

EVERYBODY IN THE GROUP HAS A SAY ON ISSUES... AND A VOTE AS WELL.

GLURTCH

CRACKK

HA HA HAA

?

CAMERA ONE

CAMERA TWO

SHRAK

SPEAKING OF GUY GARDNER, WHY WON'T YOU GUYS LET HIM BE A GREEN LANTERN ANYMORE?

WHY DID YOU FIRE HIM?

I CAN ASSURE YOU THAT WE HAD NO SAY REGARDING GUY'S STATUS IN THE GREEN LANTERN CORPS.

IT WAS *THEIR* CALL ALL THE WAY.

HUH?

BAAA!

HA HAA!

UHN! SO *FAST* I DIDN'T EVEN SEE HIM MO--

KRAKOWWW

LexOil OHIO FACILITY

SPLAKK

I WAS, Y'KNOW, WONDERIN', SUPERMAN, IF THERE'S ANYTHING OUT THERE THAT, Y'KNOW, REALLY *FRIGHTENS* YOU?

I MEAN, I'D GET SCARED FACIN' ALL THAT STUFF IF I WAS YOU.

BAH!!

UGH!

FLOOM

LexO

OHIO FA

DID YOU SEE THAT *PUNCH?!*

WHERE COULD A BEING SO POWERFUL HAVE COME *FROM?*

CAN *BLOODWYND* HAVE *SURVIVED* SOMETHING LIKE THAT?

GOOD QUESTION, MISS. SEE, ONE WAY OR ANOTHER, FEAR IS ALWAYS PART OF THE JOB.

I'M AFRAID OF FAILURE AND AFRAID OF HURTING INNOCENT PEOPLE AND, TO BE CANDID--

--I'VE BEEN AFRAID FOR MYSELF. I HAVE ENCOUNTERED THINGS POWERFUL ENOUGH TO KILL ME.

HEH.

HEH!

OH!

YOU GUYS TAKE CARE OF THE STEROID CASE! I'LL GET BLOODWYND OUT OF THAT INFERNO!

WEIRD! HERE I AM TRYING TO SAVE THE MOST MYSTERIOUS GUY IN THE LEAGUE! BLOODWYND IS HIDING SOMETHING FROM US THAT--

THERE! BUT THAT'S NOT--

OF COURSE! ALL THIS TIME I'VE WONDERED WHO BLOODWYND REALLY IS AND NOW I KNOW! I NEVER WOULD HAVE GUESSED IT IN A MILLION YEARS--

--BUT BLOODWYND IS REALLY--

45

--HAVE REPORTS OF THE JUSTICE LEAGUE BATTLING A HEINOUS MONSTER AT A LEXOIL REFINERY IN OHIO. REPORTS INDICATE THE LEAGUE IS UNABLE TO STOP HIS DESTRUCTIVE STAMPEDE.

SUPERMAN...

I HAVE TO GO.

I'M TIRED OF PLAYING TAG WITH YOU, UGLY!

LET'S SEE YOU WALK AWAY FROM A FULL-INTENSITY BLAST!

BAH!

HE'S STILL COMING! GOTTA GET MY FORCE FIELD UP BEFORE--

HA HA HAA!

AAAUHH!

THIS CREEP IS TOUGH... THAT MUCH IS OBVIOUS.

BUT RIGHT NOW ONLY *YOU* CAN SAVE TED KORD'S LIFE.

LET ME GO AFTER THE MONSTER UNTIL YOU GET BACK.

I AM A WARRIOR. IT IS AGAINST MY NATURE TO LET OTHERS DO MY WORK.

YET YOU AIDED ME IN MY STRUGGLES AGAINST STARBREAKER.

I OWE YOU *MY* AID IN RETURN.

I HOPE YOU CAN SURVIVE THE MONSTER'S WRATH UNTIL MY RETURN.

FOR NOW... BLUE BEETLE SHALL RECEIVE HIS MEDICAL CARE.

THANK YOU, MAXIMA.

BUT NOW COMES THE HARD PART!

-- EVEN THOUGH HE'S ALREADY SHREDDED THE WHOLE *TEAM!*

BUT IF I USE MY BRAINS AND KEEP MY DISTANCE I MIGHT BE ABLE TO HOLD HIM OFF UNTIL MAXIMA GETS BACK.

BOOSTER MIGHT EVEN STILL BE A HELP--

SOMEHOW I'VE GOT TO STOP THIS MANIAC BY MYSELF--

--BUT I DOUBT IT! THAT HORROR HAS PROBABLY PUT HIM IN ORBIT BY NOW!

WEIRD! IT'S TOTALLY UNYIELDING!

HE JUST MARCHES STRAIGHT AHEAD WITHOUT DEVIATING FROM HIS COURSE--NO MATTER WHAT HE FINDS IN HIS PATH!

AND IF MEMORY SERVES--

"--THERE'S A HOUSING DEVELOPMENT RIGHT OVER THAT HILL!"

MAN, DO I LOVE FRIDAYS.

NO MORE SUCKY SCHOOL FOR TWO WHOLE DAYS!

TOO BAD I GOTTA GO HOME TO THE WAR ZONE.

I CAN JUST HEAR MOM NOW. "*MITCH, DEAR, IS THAT YOU? HOW WAS YOUR DAY?*"

WHY DOES SHE ALWAYS HAVE TO BE SO CORNY?

WHAT DID SHE DO TO MAKE DAD *LEAVE* US?

HOME SWEET HOME.

WHAT A DUMP. I MEAN, I *HATE* THIS HOLE.

MITCH, DEAR, IS THAT YOU?

NO, IT'S AXL ROSE AND THE BAND.

WE GOT ANYTHING WORTH EATING AROUND HERE?

HELP YOURSELF TO THE FRIDGE. HOW WAS SCHOOL? DID YOU DO WELL ON YOUR ALGEBRA TEST?

LIKE YOU CARE.

HEY! WHAT HAPPENED TO ALL THE SODA?

OF *COURSE* I CARE. SAY, WASN'T TODAY THE DAY THAT SUPERMAN WAS GOING TO ADDRESS HIGH SCHOOL STUDENTS ON TV?

YOU MUST HAVE BEEN *THRILLED* TO SEE THAT!

NO WAY. THE SUPER WEASEL WAS CALLED AWAY ON SOME CASE SO HE BAILED EARLY.

WHY DO WE ALWAYS RUN OUT OF SODA AROUND HERE? WHY CAN'T YOU EVER *BUY* ENOUGH TO LAST?

LOOK, I'M SORRY, BUT YOUR LITTLE SISTER ISN'T FEELING WELL SO I DIDN'T HAVE *TIME* TO GO SHOPPING TODAY!

I AM REALLY TIRED OF THAT *BABY* BEING THE ONLY ONE WHO RATES AROUND HERE!

I MEAN, DAD *ALWAYS* HAS SODA FOR ME AT HIS NEW APARTMENT!

I AM SORRY, MITCHELL, BUT I CANNOT KEEP *UP* WITH EVERYTHING HERE!

THIS HOUSE ISN'T PERFECT AND NEITHER AM I BUT WE DO THE BEST WE CAN!

JEEZ.

NO WONDER DAD LEFT AND WANTS A DIVORCE.

GOIN' OVER TO AARON'S.

SEE YOU.

COOO! COOO!

WAIT! DID YOU HEAR THAT--

SKRASSH WHUMP

OH, MAN!

BECKY...! THE GLASS!

MITCHELL, I WANT YOU TO CALL 911! HURRY!

OH, GOD... OUTSIDE IN THE DRIVE-WAY...

OUR CAR!

CHECK IT OUT!

THAT DUDE DID ALL THIS-- WITH ONE HAND TIED BEHIND HIS BACK!?

HRRR?

THAT'S THE GUY, SUPERMAN. HE'S THE ONE WHO TOOK THE JUSTICE LEAGUE APART AT THE SEAMS.

WHAT WAS IT YOU CALLED HIM, BOOSTER?

OH, YEAH...

DOOMSDAY.

KRAKADOOM!

WOW! THAT PUNCH LOOKED LIKE IT COULD HAVE CAVED IN A MOUNTAIN AND SUPERMAN *TOOK* IT!

BIG DEAL, THE SPUD WAS TOO SLOW AND STUPID TO DUCK.

HURRF!

UHN!

KRAKK!

NOO...

WH--WHERE'S THE REST OF THE LEAGUE?

BRAKOOOM!

MA!

WHY? WHY ARE YOU DOING THIS TO OUR HOUSE? WHAT DO YOU WANT FROM US?

HMF...

HA!

KRUNCH!

NO! NOT MY BABY!

PLEASE, NOT MY BABY!

HMF...

POUR IT ON!

CAN'T SEE, SO SOMEBODY BETTER POINT MY RING AT THE SUCKER'S UGLY FACE!

DONE.

GIVE IT EVERYTHING YOU GOT--

MMMMM...

-- AND THIS DUDE WILL FIND OUT WHAT KIND OF TROUBLE HE BUYS WHEN HE TAKES ON THE JLA!

YOU HEARD, SUPERMAN! WE HAVE TO GET OUT OF HERE!

AND WE CAN'T LEAVE THIS POOR WOMAN IN THE LINE OF FIRE!

WOW! GUY GARDNER'S FACE IS BEATEN SO PUFFY THAT HE CAN'T EVEN SEE--

-- AND HE'S STILL IN THERE FIGHTING!

COOL!

AMAZING! I CAN'T EVEN SEE HIM ANYMORE BUT I THINK HE'S STILL STANDING!

DON'T STAND THERE BLABBIN', BLUE! JUST TURN UP THE JUICE!

GETTING TIRED...

IGNORE IT, FIRE! JUST KEEP PUSHIN'!

NO! MY FLAME IS TOTALLY SPENT!

CAN'T GO... ANYMORE!

SAME HERE!

MY POWER CELLS ARE SHOT --DRAINED!

AND WITHOUT MY SUIT'S POWERS I'M ABOUT AS POWERFUL AS PEE WEE HERMAN!

OKAY, LET'S GIVE IT A REST! AFTER ALL THIS--

--THERE'S NO WAY DOOMSDAY CAN STILL BE STANDIN'!

WITH... POWER CELLS GONE I'M IN *DEEP* TROUBLE!

FORCE FIELD-- GONE!

RRAKK

HA!

HE'S...FASTER THAN...FLASH! CAN'T GET...

SHRIIPP

RRRR

NO!

HA!

SLAMM

WHAT IS THAT-- *THING?*

CAN'T FIGHT...BUT I CAN AT LEAST *HELP* YOU!

BUT WHAT ABOUT-- *THAT?* WHAT *IS* IT?

MAYBE A ROBOT... OR *SOMETHING* FROM ANOTHER DIMENSION! WHATEVER--

"--IT'S DEADLY!"

CAN'T SEE, BUT I CAN HEAR THE BONES BREAKIN'!

GOTTA POINT... BLAST... AND HOPE!

HFFF?

HA!

UHN!

TWO-FRONT OFFENSIVE NOW!

I SHALL BLAST THIS HORROR--

UGH!

EERK!

MY EYE BEAMS!

NOOOOO!

JEEZ! BAD ENOUGH THE MONSTER IS TRASHING US! THE LEAGUE DOESN'T HAVE TO HELP!

OH, GOD... IF THAT BLAZE HAS GOTTEN TO ONE OF THE GAS LINES IN THE HOUSE...

BWHOOOOOM!

CRIPES!

TORA? TORA? ARRRR!

THUD

WHERE... WHERE IS EVERYBODY?

MA? ARE YOU OKAY?

MA?!

SO--; *KAFF*: MUCH SMOKE...

CAN'T... BREATHE, CAN'T...

HAHAHA

NO.

NO WAY--

--IS THAT MANIAC ESCAPING ME!

MA!

OH, MAN, SHE MUST BE HURT OR SOMETHING!

THE FIRE'S SURROUNDED US! I'LL NEVER GET HER OUT OF HERE!

NEED HELP...BUT THE JLA LOOKS WAY OUT OF IT OR WORSE!

"FIRE--"

"ICE--"

"--BOOSTER GOLD...THE BLOOD GUY--"

"--EVEN GUY GARDNER!"

THE ONLY ONE WHO CAN HELP US--

--HAS ALREADY BUGGED OUT AFTER THAT KILLING MACHINE!

SUPERMAN!

70

"THIS IS TOTALLY NUTS-- I COME HOME FROM SCHOOL, GET INTO ANOTHER FIGHT WITH MA..."

"...AND THEN ALL AT ONCE, THE FREAKIN' JUSTICE LEAGUE CRASHES DOWN ON US, ALONG WITH SOMEONE CALLED DOOMSDAY!"

"THE HOUSE IS A DISASTER AREA-- FLAMES ARE EVERYWHERE.

"THAT DOOMSDAY GUY DID IT ALL-- AND JUST BOOKED OUT OF HERE, WITH SUPERMAN ON HIS TAIL! *

"CAN'T HARDLY BELIEVE GUY GARDNER GOT SO BUSTED UP!

"THOSE TWO BABES, ICE AND FIRE, MIGHT BE DEAD-- I CAN'T TELL FROM HERE...

"...BUT FROM THE SOUND OF THINGS ABOUT TWENTY FEET AWAY, WHERE OUR FAMILY ROOM USED TO BE...

"...THAT BOOSTER GOLD MUST WISH HE WAS CROAKED!"

*IN SUPERMAN #74!

73

"I CAN HEAR MY MA, CALLING OUT TO ME, AND I ANSWER HER, BUT I CAN'T HELP HER OR MY BABY SISTER!"

"THROUGH THE THICK BLACK SMOKE, I SEE SUPERMAN, UP IN THE SKY--I HEAR THE SOUND OF HIS FISTS ALL OVER DOOMSDAY!"

"PLEASE, GOD--LET HIM HEAR MY CRIES FOR HELP!"

UNDER FIRE

"NO ONE ELSE CAN HELP--THE SIRENS ARE TOO FAR OFF--THEY'LL NEVER REACH US IN TIME.

"IT SEEMS LIKE THIS WHOLE DEAL HAS BEEN GOING ON FOR HOURS, THOUGH IT'S PROBABLY ONLY BEEN MINUTES!"

;KAFF KAFF; MITCH, IT'S NO USE -- I'VE GOT TO DO SOMETHING...!

74

TOM GRUMMETT—PENCILLER
DOUG HAZLEWOOD—INKER
JERRY ORDWAY—WRITER
ALBERT DE GUZMAN—LETTERER
GLENN WHITMORE—COLORIST
JENNIFER FRANK—ASSISTANT EDITOR
MIKE CARLIN—EDITOR

SUPERMAN CREATED BY SIEGEL & SHUSTER

"SMOKE'S TOO THICK--MA'S GOT TO HOLD TIGHT! I'VE GOT TO YELL LOUDER-- HE'S GOT TO HEAR ME!"

SUPERMAN! PLEASE-- YOU'VE GOT TO HELP US! MY MA'S TRAPPED-- PLEASE!

SUPERMAN-- YOU'RE THE ONLY ONE-- HELP US!

KAFF CAN'T GIVE UP-- *UGHNN* THAT KID AND HIS MOM DIDN'T ASK FOR--*

KAFF - KAFF GUY-- IT *HURTS*-- MY RIBS-- I CAN'T STAND UP TOO-- UHHN.

FOR GUY'S SAKE, I'VE GOT TO GET HIM UP-- THAT MONSTER'S ALREADY PUT BLUE BEETLE INTO A COMA.*

*ALSO IN SUPERMAN #74

MY VOICE'S GOING-- FROM BREATHIN' THIS SMOKE-- BUT I'VE GOTTA KEEP YELLIN'! UNLESS HE'S NOT *LISTENING?*

NAH, HE'S A HERO-- THEY'RE *SUPPOSED* TO HELP US! MAYBE THAT *DOOMSDAY'S BEATING SUPERMAN?* WHAT DO I DO THEN?

HELP US, SUPERMAN-- PLEASE!

I HEAR YOU, KID-- I JUST THOUGHT ONE OF THE LEAGUERS MIGHT BE ABLE TO--!

DAMN! GARDNER AND THE REST ARE UNCONSCIOUS! I'VE GOT TO GET BACK DOWN THERE!

"THEY'RE SO HIGH UP, BUT IT LOOKS LIKE--THAT'S IT--THAT'S IT-- HE'S LOOKING THIS WAY."

"HE SEES ME!"

¡WHU-UHHHFF!¡

GWAM

"SHOOT! THAT SOUNDED LIKE THUNDER! SUPIE'S GOTTA SHAKE THAT DOOMSDAY CRUD BEFORE HE CAN DO US ANY GOOD!"

THIS CREATURE'S FAST, AND STRONG-- BUT IT SEEMS TO LEAP RATHER THAN FLY.

SO LONG AS I CAN HOLD TIGHT--IT'S AT MY MERCY WHERE INERTIA'S INVOLVED!

77

I'VE GOT TO FORCE THIS *THING* FAR ENOUGH INTO THE LAKE'S SILT...

CHOOM

"...AND *HOPE* IT'S SOFT ENOUGH TO KEEP HIM FROM USING IT TO PROPEL HIMSELF FOR A FEW MINUTES!"

"I JUST *PRAY* I'VE STILL GOT *TIME* TO HELP THAT FAMILY!"

KERACK

OH, *MERCY*-- DON'T LET THAT BE THE SOUND OF THOSE BEAMS GIVING WAY!

:UGHNN: HOPE IS *NOT* LOST...

"...NOT WHILE *BLOODWYND* STILL STANDS!"

I DON'T KNOW WHERE YOU CAME FROM, MISTER-- BUT THANK GOD YOU'RE *HERE*!

78

YOU AND YOUR CHILD SHOULD ALSO THANK SUPERMAN.

BLOODWYND-- ARE YOU OKAY? YOU TOOK QUITE A BEATING--

ALL OF THE LEAGUERS DID-- BUT THIS GUY KEEPS SURPRISING ME WITH HIS--RESILIENCY.

S-SUPERMAN-- WHAT ABOUT MY SON, MITCH?

HE'S DOWN THERE WITH THE E.M.S. CREW, MISS.

THEY DID IT! THEY SAVED MY MOM AND MY BABY SISTER!

YOU SHOULD GO TO THE HOSPITAL-- YOU ALL TOOK IN A LOT OF SMOKE.

GUY-- LIE STILL.

HOW 'BOUT IT, FELLA? LET'S HAVE A LOOK AT YOU.

NO. I DESIRE NO MEDICAL TREATMENT.

I WISH TO BE ALONE.

ODD-- BLOODWYND'S TELEPORTED RATHER THAN SEEK TREATMENT--!

DON'T STRUGGLE-- WHAT IS IT?

"KAFF KAFF! DON'T WUSS OUT, BOYSCOUT! PUT THIS DOOMSDAY GUY IN A PINE BOX--

--OR I'LL CRAWL OFFA THIS GURNEY AND KICK BOTH O' YER BUTTS! ::KAFF::"

I'LL TAKE CARE OF THINGS, GUY-- YOU JUST LET THE DOCTORS HELP YOU!

YOU THERE-- HAVE YOUR LOCAL HOSPITAL CONTACT MAXWELL LORD IN NEW YORK CITY FOR THESE FOLKS' MEDICAL RECORDS!

NOW TO SEE IF THIS "DOOMSDAY" IS STILL WHERE I LEFT HIM!

"QUESTION IS-- HOW DO I RESTRAIN HIM WHEN THE COMBINED FORCE OF THE JUSTICE LEAGUE COULDN'T DO IT?"

HOLY--! THAT'S OUR TARGET DOWN THERE, RALPH!

IT'S COMING UP FAST, BUT OUR WEAPONS SYSTEM'S LOCKED ON! COMMENCING LAUNCH OF HELLFIRES--

SPLASH!

80

SOMETHING TORE UP A STRETCH OF PROPERTY OUT ON ROUTE 110, RUSTY!

KIRBY COUNTY POLICE

LOWELL SAID A BUNCH OF FOLK--INCLUDING SOME OF THE JUSTICE LEAGUE --ARE BEING RUSHED TO THE HOSPITAL!

SAY, YOU HEAR THAT? KIND OF A CARTOON SOUND A BOMB MAKES JUST BEFORE IT--

SHOULD I CRANK UP THE CIVIL DEFENSE SIREN, CHIEF? MAYBE WE SHOULD GET EVERYONE INTO THEIR BASEMENTS--

MOTHER OF PEARL!

CRASHH!

UH, CHIEF-- THINK I'M GONNA NEED A BIGGER GUN!

KIRBY COUNTY POLICE STATION

LOOK, MR. VICE-LIEUTENANT GOVERNOR-- I'M TELLING YOU THIS IS GOING TO BE MORE THAN "JUST" A LOCAL EMERGENCY...

...IF'N YOU DON'T GET THE BLASTED NATIONAL GUARD HERE A.S.A.P.!

SKAAASH

MOTHER O' MERCY! YOU HEAR THAT, YOU TIN-HORN BUREAUCRAT?

THIS IS BLUE LEADER-- TARGET SIGHTED AND WE'RE READY FOR A RUN. OVER.

THWACK

BLUE LEADER-- APPROACH WITH EXTREME CAUTION-- WE'VE ALREADY LOST ONE CHOPPER TO THIS THING! OVER.

POK POK POK

WE HEAR YA, CONTROL. OVER AND OUT.

MAIN ST.

RRRANK

THWOCK

THIS "BUBBA'S" TAKING EVERYTHING THE CHAIN GUN'S RAINING ON HIM WITH A SMILE!

CHANK

WHAT THE--? WE'VE BEEN HIT!

NO... WE'VE BEEN SPEARED...

THE BACK-UP CONTROL SYSTEM'S NOT GONNA DO SQUAT WITH "BUBBA" DOWN THERE DIRECTING OUR FLIGHT!

HO-LEEEEE-- NO TIME TO BAIL! MAYDAY MAYDAY!

HI, "TURTLE-BOY."

WHAT'S GOING ON?

JIMMY-- THE CHIEF WILL HAVE YOUR *HIDE!* YOUR LUNCH HOUR ISN'T *THREE HOURS* LONG!

LOIS!

ERR, TAPING RAN A LITTLE LONG, BUT THIS IS MY FIRST TV SHOW.

WHY ARE YOU *WHISPERING?*

PERRY WANTS US TO COVER THIS *"DOOMSDAY"* INCIDENT. NED'S WAITING FOR US AT THE *HELI-PAD!* HURRY *UP!*

YOU TWO BETTER LOOK AT SOMETHING *FIRST.* GBS IS ABOUT TO INTERRUPT "THE BRAVE AND THE BOLD" FOR A *NEWSBREAK.*

COME *ON,* "TURTLE-BOY!"

THAT'S *MISTER* "TURTLE-BOY" TO YOU.

SURE, FINE. JUST *LEAVE* BEFORE WE'RE FINISHED, WHY DON'T YOU?

HI, LEON. MIND IF WE WATCH?

NOPE.

THIS IS A *GBS NEWSBREAK.* I'M STEVE LOMBARD.

THE DESTRUCTIVE FORCE KNOWN AS *"DOOMSDAY"* HAS LEFT *THIRTY DEAD* IN ITS WAKE...

...HUNDREDS HAVE BEEN INJURED, INCLUDING MEMBERS OF THE FAMED *JUSTICE LEAGUE.*

DOOMSDAY

IT APPEARS *"DOOMSDAY"* IS ON A STRAIGHT PATH CROSSING FROM *OHIO* THROUGH *NEW YORK STATE...*

...SOME THEORIZE THAT THE CREATURE IS ON A COURSE STRAIGHT TO--OR THROUGH-- METROPOLIS.

"WE NOW RETURN YOU TO "THE BRAVE AND THE BOLD," ALREADY IN PROGRESS.

BLOODY--!

LEX, I SHOULD GO-- MAYBE I CAN LEND A HAND.

THERE'S GOT TO BE A MILLION THINGS I COULD--

LISTEN, LOVE--YOU CAN'T JUST UP AND RUN OFF LIKE YOU DID DURING THAT SATANUS BUSINESS.

I NEED MY SUPERGIRL HERE WITH ME...

"...WE NEED A CONTINGENCY PLAN IN CASE THIS MENACE MAKES HIS WAY TO METROPOLIS."

BY THE HOUSE OF ALMERAC--YOU STILL STAND, EH?

YOU WILL
BOW DOWN
BEFORE ME,
CREATURE!

KRAAAAAASH

GOOD FOOD
YOU BETCHA!

MAXIMA?
WHAT ON
EARTH?

THERE'RE
BOUND TO BE
PEOPLE IN
THAT STORE...

THERE ARE
ALWAYS
INNOCENT
VICTIMS IN
BATTLE!

DO NOT DARE TO
IMPUGN ME, SUPERMAN!

LOOK, JUST
THINK BEFORE
YOU SWING, OKAY,
PRINCESS? WE
CAN'T QUARREL
AMONG OUR--

THWACK!

-UGHNN!-

WAM

YOUR *ONSLAUGHT* DOES LITTLE BUT *STIMULATE* ME, CREATURE!

MAXIMA WELCOMES THIS, FOR ONLY WHEN A WARRIOR FACES DEATH CAN A CONFLICT BE DEEMED TRULY *WORTHY!*

MAXIE'S REVELING IN THIS, AND DOOMSDAY DOESN'T SEEM TO BE SLOWING DOWN MUCH....

SLAM

KA-BOOM

....BUT I DON'T KNOW HOW MUCH *LONGER* I CAN KEEP *THIS UP!*

FOR THE TIME BEING, I'D BETTER WORRY ABOUT ALL THIS GASOLINE *GUSHING* UP!

HOLD HIM *TIGHT,* KRYPTONIAN-- MAXIMA WILL *NOT MISS AGAIN!*

MAXIMA! THAT LIGHT POLE'S GOING TO *SPARK!*

SPAK!

"NOTHING COULD'VE PREPARED ME FOR THE SIGHT THAT GREETED ME."

"THE TOWN'S MAIN STREET WAS DEVASTATED, WITH DEBRIS STREWN EVERYWHERE."

"IT WAS AS IF A HURRICANE HAD SWEPT THROUGH... AND IN A WAY, ONE HAD."

"THE MEDIA HAD A NAME FOR IT-- DOOMSDAY."

SUPERMAN-- FRIEND--CAN YOU HEAR ME?

WAS ALL THIS NECESSARY--THIS DESTRUCTION?

G-GUARDIAN?

MAXIMA--?

SHE'S STARTING TO STIR-- I THINK SHE'LL BE OKAY.

WASN'T THERE SOME OTHER WAY?

THERE ALWAYS IS, BUT THAT DOESN'T ALTER THE FACT THAT I'VE STILL GOT TO STOP HIM...

...AND NOW I REALIZE I HAVE TO DO IT ALONE!

... DOOMSDAY IS NEAR!

A BATTLE THAT HAS RAGED ACROSS HALF THE NATION SINCE MIDDAY, HAS LEFT SEVERAL MEMBERS OF JUSTICE LEAGUE AMERICA SERIOUSLY INJURED.

THE BLUE BEETLE IS REPORTED TO BE COMATOSE, AND BOOSTER GOLD SERIOUSLY INJURED FOLLOWING ... ONE MOMENT!

SPECIAL REPORT

THIS JUST HANDED ME ... THE VILLAGE OF GRIFFITH IN UPSTATE KIRBY COUNTY WAS ROCKED BY AN EXPLOSION MOMENTS AGO, AS SUPERMAN AND MAXIMA FOUGHT TO STOP THE CREATURE-- DUBBED DOOMSDAY--

CAMCORDER FOOTAGE

--WHOSE RAMPAGE HAS BROKEN THE JLA AND LEFT A TRAIL OF DEATH AND DESTRUCTION BEHIND HIM. DESPITE THEIR EFFORTS, HOWEVER, THE CREATURE IS REPORTEDLY STILL ON THE LOOSE.

CIVIL DEFENSE UNITS IN CITIES ALL ALONG THE EASTERN SEABOARD ARE ON ALERT, AS AUTHORITIES TRY TO DETERMINE IF ...

DOOMSDAY... MUST STOP DOOMSDAY...

PLEASE, MAXIMA... TAKE IT SLOW AND EASY. YOU'VE SUFFERED A PRETTY SERIOUS CONCUSSION.

SORRY I DIDN'T GET HERE SOONER, SUPERMAN.

I DOUBT THAT YOU COULD HAVE HELPED US AVOID THIS, GUARDIAN.

WE'VE NEVER FACED ANYTHING QUITE LIKE THIS BEFORE.

ROGER STERN • JACKSON GUICE & DENIS RODIER
WRITER   ARTISTS

BILL   GLENN   JENNIFER   MIKE
OAKLEY   •   WHITMORE   •   FRANK   •   CARLIN
LETTERER   COLORIST   ASSISTANT   EDITOR

SUPERMAN created by JERRY SIEGEL & JOE SHUSTER

95

MAXIMA'S RIGHT... DOOMSDAY MUST BE *STOPPED!* HE'S A THREAT TO EVERY LIVING THING!

BUT SHE'S IN NO CONDITION TO DEAL WITH HIM.

GET HER TO A *HOSPITAL,* GUARDIAN.

I'LL STOP DOOMSDAY... IF IT'S THE LAST THING I DO!

MY GOD... LOOK AT THAT!

TRACKING DOOMSDAY IS LIKE FOLLOWING THE PATH OF A *TORNADO...* THERE'S UTTER DEVASTATION EVERYWHERE HE TOUCHES DOWN.

THERE ARE A HALF-DOZEN MAJOR URBAN CENTERS IN THIS REGION... OVER 25 MILLION HUMAN LIVES ENDANGERED BY THAT MONSTER!

I WISH I KNEW WHERE DOOMSDAY CAME FROM...

"...I'VE NEVER SEEN ANY-THING--

KTOOM

"--ON EARTH OR OFF IT-- TO EQUAL HIM FOR SHEER BRUTE STRENGTH!

"IT WAS PAINFUL TO SEE WHAT HE'D DONE TO GUY GARDNER.

FRAKAMM!

"IF ANYTHING, HE'S MORE SINGLE-MINDED THAN DRAAGA WAS... AND HE SEEMS EVEN MORE IRRATIONAL THAN LOBO, IF THAT'S POSSIBLE."

GRAUHRRR!

"THERE'S A FRIGHTENING THOUGHT. LOBO'S GIVEN ME A HARD TIME MORE THAN ONCE... BUT LOBO'S POWER, HIS RAGE, DOESN'T BEGIN TO COMPARE TO DOOMSDAY'S!

"THERE'S NO DISCERNIBLE PATTERN TO HIS MOVEMENTS--"

MY GOD, THE OVERPASS HAS COLLAPSED!

WHAT'S THAT COMING OUT--?

NO! CAN'T STOP IN TIME! I'M GONNA HIT--

HRAURR!

--HIM! HUH? HE....?

WHAT DID--? HOW DID HE--?

OMIGOD... I DON'T BELIEVE THIS!

I'M.... FLYING?

"-- HE JUST SEEMS TO WANDER FROM PLACE TO PLACE, ATTACKING WHAT-EVER CATCHES HIS EYE."

RAURR?

CREATURE? I...YEAH! HE... WAS *BIG*... CAME RIGHT AT ME. H-HE GRABBED HOLD OF MY CAR AND JUST... *THREW* IT!

IT HAPPENED SO FAST... DIDN'T SEEM REAL AT FIRST. WHAT... WHAT *IS* HE, SUPERMAN?

I WISH I KNEW. HE CAME FROM OUT OF NOWHERE -- DESTROYING THINGS AT RANDOM -- APPARENTLY FOR THE SHEER HELL OF IT!

THEN.... YEAH... IT MUSTA BEEN *HIM* THAT COLLAPSED THE OVERPASS!

OVERPASS?!

"DAMN. I DON'T SEE ANY SURVIVORS AMONG THE WRECKAGE.

"LOOKS LIKE THERE'RE DOZENS OF CHAIN-REACTION FENDER-BENDERS UP AND DOWN BOTH HIGHWAYS... LOTS OF MINOR INJURIES THERE.

"AH -- THERE'S A STATE TROOPER ON THE SCENE. GOOD. AND I HEAR RESCUE VEHICLES ON THE WAY--!"

OH, NO!

WHAT'S WRONG? WHAT DO YOU SEE?

MORE TROUBLE... *TERRIBLE* TROUBLE.

I'M NEEDED--! I'LL SET YOU DOWN NEAR THAT STATE TROOPER.

TELL HER TO CALL FOR MORE RESCUE TEAMS! WE'LL NEED THEM--

DOOMSDAY!!

URRGH?

KTOOM!

HOLY--! WHAT WAS *THAT*?!

I ... I THINK THE RED-AN'- BLUE BLUR IS SUPERMAN. I DON'T WANNA KNOW WHAT THE OTHER THING IS!

AMSCRAY, YOU TWO! WE GOTTA EVACUATE THIS LOADIN' DOCK--ON THE DOUBLE!

HAH-HA-HAH-HA-HA!

OW! THIS IS... INSANE!

I'D SWEAR... THE HARDER I FIGHT... THE MORE DOOMSDAY LIKES IT!

HE'S BEEN FIGHTING MOST OF THE DAY, BUT HE STILL SEEMS AS EAGER--AND AS STRONG-- AS EVER!

IF HE HAS ENERGY RESERVES AS EXTENSIVE AS MINE, I MAY BE IN TROUBLE!

WUP-WUP-WUP!

EH? 'COPTERS...

...THE ONE IN THE LEAD IS THE DAILY PLANET'S FLYING NEWSROOM--

"--OH, LORD, AND LOIS AND JIMMY ARE ON BOARD! I HOPE THE PILOT KEEPS HIS DISTANCE!"

THAT'S DOOMSDAY? WOW, HE'S A BIG ONE!

VERY BIG. BE CAREFUL, CLARK.

"...THE MIDVALE LEX-MART STOOD IN RUINS AS SUPERMAN STRUGGLED WITH THE MYSTERIOUS CREATURE." END OF PARAGRAPH...

"...STAND BY FOR MORE."

WLEX LIVE

WELL, MY *NEWS DIRECTOR* ASSURED ME THAT HE'D DISPATCHED A CAMERA CREW TO GET TO THE BOTTOM OF THIS *DOOMSDAY NONSENSE*...

...SO YOU WON'T GO CHASING OFF AFTER IT, LIKE YOU DID DURING THAT *SATANUS AFFAIR.* *

IT'S NOT NONSENSE, LEX! THEY'RE ON THE AIR *NOW*-- DOOMSDAY JUST WRECKED ONE OF YOUR *SHOPPING MARTS!*

*IN ISSUE # 680.

WHAT?! BLOODY HELL!

SUPERMAN'S *TRYING* TO STOP THE CREATURE, BUT HE'S NOT HAVING MUCH LUCK.

ANYTHING THAT CAN GIVE SUPERMAN THAT HARD A FIGHT MUST BE INCREDIBLY POWERFUL! I'D BETTER GO HELP--!

WE'VE BEEN ALL THROUGH THAT, LOVE! THE *LAST* THING WE NEED NOW IS FOR YOU TO GO FLYING OFF! WHENEVER SUPERMAN'S AWAY, THE LOCAL CITIZENRY START GETTING... *EDGY*...

...I DON'T LIKE IT, BUT I CAN'T DENY IT--

--AND WITH THE OL' BOY OFF HAVIN' A GO-ROUND WITH SOME UGLY *DRONGO*, THE CITY NEEDS ITS *SUPERGIRL* TO FILL THE VOID.

ARE YOU *SURE*, LEX? DOOMSDAY'S ALREADY CAUSED SO MUCH DESTRUCTION. AND YOUR NEWSMAN PLACED THE LATEST *DEATH TOLL* AT OVER A *HUNDRED!*

WLEX LIVE

SUPERMAN CAN HANDLE HIM, AND *I* CAN WEATHER THE LOSS OF A LEX-MART! TRUST ME, PET, THE GOOD PEOPLE OF METROPOLIS WILL FEEL BETTER KNOWING THAT YOU AND TEAM-LUTHOR ARE HOME.

ALL RIGHT, I'LL STAY... FOR NOW!

AS IF SUPERMAN EVER *REALLY* NEEDS HELP! HE'S *ALWAYS* SURVIVED... DESPITE MY BEST-LAID PLANS!

YOU'LL SEE, LOVE--

"--SUPERMAN WILL BE JUST FINE!"

"THEIR BATTLE RAGED ON ACROSS THE REAR LOT OF A FAST FOOD RESTAURANT, WHERE-- OMIGOD!

Welcome to

...j Bel

BURG[

BUS PARKI[

"UH...WHERE D-DOOMSDAY HURLED A PARKED *BUS* AT THE MAN OF STEEL...

"...KNOCKING HIM THROUGH THE SIDE OF A BUILDING."

LOOK OUT!

WHAT--?

INCOMING! EVERYBODY DOWN!

HAH-HA!

AT LEAST...THE BUS...WAS *EMPTY.* BUT...ALL THOSE PEOPLE...INSIDE THE RESTAURANT--! HOPE THEY'RE... ALL RIGHT.

GOT TO... PULL MYSELF... TOGETHER.

GOT TO... END THIS...

GEEZ! SUPERMAN MUST'VE GOTTEN A SECOND WIND OR SOMETHING! I'VE NEVER SEEN HIM FIGHT SO HARD!

N-NEITHER HAVE I, JIMMY!

NEXT PARAGRAPH... "TAKING ADVANTAGE OF THE CREATURE'S MOMENTARY DISTRACTION--

"--SUPERMAN REDOUBLED HIS EFFORTS..."

GOT TO KEEP HIM OFF-BALANCE-- AND AVOID HIS REACH! HE MUST WEIGH CLOSE TO A TON...

...GOT TO USE THAT WEIGHT... BUILD UP ENOUGH MOMENTUM...

...TO HURL HIM AWAY FROM HERE... AWAY FROM METROPOLIS!

DOOMSDAY'S TAKEN EVERYTHING I'VE DISHED OUT SO FAR... MAYBE SLAMMING INTO THE HILLS AT A FEW HUNDRED MILES PER HOUR WILL SOFTEN HIM UP!

I HOPE SO! THIS IS ONE TIME I COULD REALLY USE SOME *HELP...* AND THE JLA IS INCAPACITATED!

I'M SURPRISED THAT YOUNG LEX LUTHOR HASN'T SENT SUPERGIRL TO HELP-- BY NOW HE SURELY KNOWS ABOUT DOOMSDAY SMASHING HIS STORE!

LEX THE SECOND IS A MORE ACTIVE TYPE THAN HIS FATHER WAS... I'D HALF-EXPECT HIM TO LEAD A *TEAM-LUTHOR* SQUADRON UP HERE *HIMSELF!*

OF COURSE, IF HIS *FATHER* WERE STILL ALIVE, I'D HAVE HALF-EXPECTED THE OLD MAN TO HAVE *ENGINEERED* THIS DOOMSDAY MONSTER!

I DON'T KNOW IF I CAN CATCH UP WITH THEM, MS. LANE, NOT AS FAST AS THEY'RE GOING!

JUST DO YOUR BEST, GARRET.

METROPOLIS ISN'T THAT FAR... I'LL BET SUPER-MAN'S TRYING TO KEEP DOOMSDAY AWAY FROM THE CITY.

WELL, HE'S HEADED IN THE RIGHT DIRECTION...

"... NOT MUCH TO WORRY ABOUT THERE. NO ONE'S ALLOWED MUCH UP INTO THOSE HILLS.

BUH-BOOM!

"EVEN A LOT OF THE *AIR-SPACE* IS RESTRICTED...

"... I THINK SOME SORT OF FEDERAL PRESERVE IS TUCKED AWAY UP THERE."

BUH-BOOM!

CADMUS PROJECT

©#*%!! WHAT'S GOING ON?! IS THIS AN *EARTHQUAKE?!*

INCONCEIVABLE! THIS IS ONE OF THE MOST *GEOPHYSICALLY STABLE* REGIONS ON THE CONTINENT! NO...

...THE PROJECT MUST BE UNDER SOME MANNER OF *BOMBARDMENT!*

TAKE IT EASY, WESTFIELD! WE'LL GET TO THE BOTTOM OF THIS.

YES... YES, YOU'RE RIGHT, JOHNSON... WE *MUST!*

THE GUARDIAN *WOULD* HAVE TO BE AWAY! THIS IS INORDINATELY INOPPORTUNE... UNLESS... YOU DON'T SUPPOSE--? NO, THE LEVEL OF COINCIDENCE IS FAR TOO GREAT...

"... AND YET, I CANNOT HELP BUT WONDER IF THIS SEISMIC DISRUPTION IS SOMEHOW RELATED TO THAT NEARBY MONSTER SCARE WHICH THE GUARDIAN IS INVESTIGATING."

UHHN... HHUNGH...

* THE TREE-CITY GROWN BY CREATIONS OF THE CADMUS PROJECT. SUPERMAN WAS LAST HERE IN THE LANDMARK *ACTION COMICS* #655.

"--THEIR GENETICS LABS HAVE CREATED ALL MANNER OF BEINGS."

I THINK MAXIMA WILL BE OKAY... AS HARD A TIME AS SHE WAS GIVING THE DOCTORS--!

NEEP. NEEP. NEEP!

EH? THE ALERT SIGNAL? NOW WHAT?!

GUARDIAN-- RETURN TO BASE AT ONCE!

WHAT IS IT, RODRIGUES? WHAT'S WRONG?

UNKNOWN. THE MOUNTAIN SEEMS TO BE UNDER ATTACK--

"-- BY FORCES OF INCREDIBLE POWER!"

THIS ¿ UNNGH ¿ IS NOT ¿ OW ¿ GETTING ANY EASIER! JUST HITTING DOOMSDAY HURTS... AND HE DOESN'T SEEM... TO HAVE WEAKENED... ONE IOTA!

HRAH-HAH-HA!

THIS IS... JUST WEARING... ME DOWN. GOT TO... CHANGE MY TACTICS.

MAYBE IF I... HIT HIM WITH SOMETHING...

...Y-E-A-H... SOMETHING BIG!

THESE SUPPORT COLUMNS... MAY BE ORGANIC... BUT THEY'RE HARD... AS TEMPERED STEEL!

HHUNK!

WORTH A TRY--!

PTOOM!

GUARDIAN TO BASE! HABITAT... MY GOD, HABITAT IS COLLAPSING -- LIKE A HOUSE OF CARDS!

AND SUPERMAN AND THAT MONSTER ARE SMACK IN THE MIDDLE OF IT!

I-IT'S BAD... I'M GOING IN FOR A CLOSER LOOK! I'LL KEEP THIS CHANNEL OPEN...

KLANNG!

"NEGATIVE, FRAN. THE PLANET'S CHOPPER IS CHASING DOOMSDAY AS FAST AS IT CAN...

"...CAT GRANT'S WGBS CHOPPER IS ACCOMPANYING US...

HRARRH!

"...BUT SUPERMAN IS ON THE CREATURE'S TAIL."

"KEEP YOUR HEAD DOWN, FRAN. IF OUR CALCULATIONS ARE RIGHT, THAT MONSTER MUST BE REACHING METROPOLIS ABOUT NOW!"

DOOMSDAY
IS HERE!

FORGET IT, DOOMSDAY! YOUR RAMPAGE STOPS HERE!

STORY:
LOUISE SIMONSON
PENCILLER:
JON BOGDANOVE
INKER:
DENNIS JANKE
LETTERER:
BILL OAKLEY
COLORIST:
GLENN WHITMORE
ASSISTANT EDITOR:
JENNIFER FRANK
EDITOR:
MIKE CARLIN

SUPERMAN created by
JERRY SIEGEL and JOE SHUSTER

HURH?!

KLIK-WRRR.
KLIK-WRRR

WE'VE *GOT* HIM, *FRAN!* NEW *PARAGRAPH:*

"DOOMSDAY'S RAMPAGE IN PARK RIDGE WAS CUT SHORT WHEN SUPERMAN GRABBED THE MONSTER...

"...ROCKETING HIM AWAY FROM METROPOLIS, TOWARD THE VACUUM OF SPACE." END OF PARAGRAPH.

AN' IF HE KNOWS WHAT'S *GOOD* FOR HIM, HE'LL *STAY* THERE.

I... *HOPE* SO, JOE. DOOMSDAY IS PROBABLY THE *DEADLIEST* FOE SUPERMAN HAS EVER FACED.

MAN, THIS MUST BE MY *LUCKY YEAR.* THOSE WERE SOME OF THE *BEST* SHOTS I'VE EVER GOTTEN.

DON'T *SWEAT* IT, LOIS. HE'S *SUPERMAN,* RIGHT--

"--HE'S GOTTA BE OKAY!"

GUARDIAN, ARE YOU ALL RIGHT?

DUBBILEX! WHAT... HAPPENED?

DOOMS-DAY SMASHED HABITAT! YOU WERE FELLED BY THE RUBBLE.

AND SUPER-MAN...?

EVEN NOW HE BATTLES THE CREATURE.

I'M AFRAID DOOMSDAY IS TOO BIG FOR SUPERMAN TO HANDLE ALONE.

DOOMSDAY MAY BE ONE OF OURS, GUARDIAN, A D.N.ALIEN... A CADMUS-DABNEY DONOVAN CREATION.

TRY TO MIND-READ THE CREATURE, DUB. FIND OUT. I JUST PRAY THAT CADMUS ISN'T RESPONSIBLE--

"--FOR THE DAMAGE THAT MONSTER'S CAUSED!"

WHACK

CREATURE'S AS AGILE... AS IT IS STRONG! TWISTED AWAY ...COULDN'T HOLD HIM...

KICKED ME... CAN'T BREATHE...

THERE IS NOTHING IN HIS MIND BUT ANGER--

123

"--TO FOLLOW HIS PATH OF DESTRUCTION."

KRRKT

THOMB

THE CEILING!

WATCH OUT!

WHAT THAT BE?

WHAT CRASH THROUGH TO UNDERWORLD?!

BIG SUCKER!

MAYBE COMIN' TA RESCUE THE PRISONERS?

THAT'S WHAT YOU FOOLS GET FOR DARING TO PUT WARWORLDERS ON TRIAL!!

hurf! <SMELL--> <--GAS?>

CRA KSH

TK-TK! <WHO CARE WHAT HE SMELL LIKE, KR'LI?! PLUG UGLY'S OUR TICKET TO FREEDOM!> TK-TK!

MY LORD IN HEAVEN! HE'S THROWN OFF *SUPERMAN!*

WHAT-- WHAT *IS* THAT CREATURE?

I SUS-PECT IT'S A *DOOMSDAY WEAPON,* MILDRED...

...LEFT BEHIND BY *WARWORLD* TO *DECI-MATE* THE EARTH IN CASE THEIR SWARM FAILED!

BLASH

WE FINALLY GOT DIS *LASER CANNON* SHOVED UP ON DA ROOF O' YOUR LAB, PER-FESSER HAM...

...SO LET'S *USE* IT!!

AS SOON AS *SUPERGIRL* GETS OUT OF THE WAY, BIBBO!

YOU AND MILDRED KEEP YOUR *FORCE BELTS* BUCKLED TIGHT!

WHEN THE CREATURE FEELS THE *BLAST,* HE'S GOING TO BE ANGRY!

NEVER SEEN A CREATURE THIS *POWERFUL.* MUST BE SOME--

DOOMSDAY!

DAN JURGENS / BRETT BREEDING
Words & Pictures / Finished Art

JOHN COSTANZA / GLENN WHITMORE
Letters / Colors

JENNIFER FRANK / MIKE CARLIN
Assistant / Editor

SUPERMAN created by
JERRY SIEGEL & JOE SHUSTER

144

145

146

149

"It's fresh air. I like this all-too-human Superman, and I think a lot of you will, too."
—SCRIPPS HOWARD NEWS SERVICE

START AT THE BEGINNING!

SUPERMAN: ACTION COMICS VOLUME 1: SUPERMAN AND THE MEN OF STEEL

SUPERMAN VOLUME 1: WHAT PRICE TOMORROW?

SUPERGIRL VOLUME 1: THE LAST DAUGHTER OF KRYPTON

SUPERBOY VOLUME 1: INCUBATION

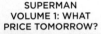